The Hospice Bubble
& Other Devastating Affirmations

by Lizzie Wann

Lizzie Wann

For Steve —
Hearing your stories
made me want to share
mine with you. All the best

Published by Puna Press
P.O. Box 7790, San Diego, CA 92167
www.punapress.com

Copyright © 2019 Lizzie Wann

All rights reserved. No part of this book may be reproduced, stored in a retrieval system, or transmitted in any form, or by any means electronic, mechanical, photocopying, recording or otherwise, without permission in writing from the publisher.

Art by David Dickey

Printed in the United States of America
by EC Printing
ecprinting.com

Thank you.

Library of Congress Control Number: 2018950859

ISBN: 978-0-9983728-3-9

To Mom & Sandy. We did it right.
And to Dad. You knew all along.

Contents

The Hospice Bubble

1. Patricia Said
2. In a Train Station in Chicago, Sunday Morning, 1961
3. Nothing But Happy
4. Dad's Wisdom
5. Letters in the Air
6. Winter Solstice 2017
7. Hospice Bubble Haiku
8. Lift Team
9. Poem from Inside His Hands
10. Christmas Day
11. The Magical Cheeseburger
13. Caregiving
15. Bequeathments
16. New Year's Eve/New Year's Day
18. The Day He Died
19. The Hospice Bubble
20. No Funeral
21. A Proper Heaven
23. Picking Up the Ashes
24. Lung Point
25. This is a True Story

Other Devastating Affirmations

Death

28. Dixon, CA Pop. 13,708
29. Great Uncle
30. Coming Rains
31. Swimming in the Sky
32. Sky Search
33. For Jeff Buckley
34. To a Ghost
35. My Ophelia

Depression

38. Lessons
39. Breaking the Weather
40. A Girl I Know

41. How to Bring Her Back
42. Hole in the Floor Mat
43. Break
44. Phantoms & Flights
45. Hawks & Sunsets
46. Moon Shine
48. Bone Songs
49. Murders, Unkindnesses & Other Winged Things
50. No Man's Land
51. December Sleep
52. Figure at a Window, 1925
53. Emergence

Writing

56. One Way Rain
57. Poet Out of Practice
58. Grace
59. Best Poem I Ever Wrote
60. Letter to a Blue Moon

Love

62. Close
63. Camouflage
64. A Hard Cry Could Draw Walls In
65. Novice Masons
66. Contractors
67. Master Builders
68. Holidays
69. The Girl Who Dreamed of Bees
70. The Ballad of Richard & Mildred
72. Sins & Miracles
73. Aero-Dynamics
74. My Pleasure
75. Letter Writing #1
76. Letter Writing #3
77. Letter Writing #5
78. Midnight Lesson
79. The Window
80. The Breath Before Hallelujah
81. Season's End

The Hospice Bubble

Patricia Said...
(a birthday poem for my father)

Patricia said her daddy read her newspaper stories at bedtime
so she became a reporter

you took me on interstate trips,
skirting company policy of no passengers
& I have become this

Patricia said in half-dark, she would stand on her father's feet
& they danced in the kitchen
we have done this too

Patricia said he taught her how to make hot water cornbread
you also have cooked for me,
chocolate chip waffles for breakfast at noon on Sundays
& I used to sit on ice cream maker as you hand-cranked it
enormous salt crystals spilled out as you added them to brew
on hot August afternoons in that dry
Snake River hometown of mine

Patricia said he is dead now, taken by a bullet in a robbery
she grew into his legacy for language

you are alive & a year older
& have no bones to pick with me

Patricia said she whispered against his cheek
about a boy's first kiss in their
hot skillet cornbread kitchen
you have never inquired about boys, or men for that matter

but in that silence of griddle ready for batter
& ice cream almost perfect
& feel of your work boots that I helped unlace
under my own child feet
hand in hand, we stepped in a dance

now I say, Patricia, we girls own the purest love
& know the best dancers

In a Train Station in Chicago, Sunday Morning, 1961

he travels cross country by train
it pulls into Chicago at dawn
he is a young man
he is going home to California
he does not know this city

he tells me this story many years later
after my own visit to Chicago
after I tell him that riding the 'el' train
back & forth
seemed to sharpen
city's edge

Chicago took something from me
satisfied something too

I sometimes believe
I could be Patsy Cline
singing songs of heartache & loneliness
that remind people like him
about a Sunday morning
in a train station in a city he did not know

he tells me that everything-
that station, that city, that morning-
was lonesome
how he can't hear Johnny Cash sing
"Sunday Mornin' Comin' Down"
without thinking of Chicago

I can't listen to his stories
without finding poetry

Nothing But Happy

with an uncommonly clear
Los Angeles horizon before me
air that smelled of ocean
I felt like I was in a movie
but I wasn't acting a part
neither was he

we were bound together
in a moment that smacked of reality
life's seriousness
a relationship's depth & knowledge
were distilled into a quiet hour
like fluids dripping into his veins

a man at odds with his own body
no reason, no explanation
just in a bed, in a hospital room
medicine working silently

steamed vegetables & dry turkey
shots of potassium mixed with cranberry juice
he with a desire, an urgency
to talk to me
to tell me he loves me
to tell me how he feels

he spoke of how he never knew that on September 24,
41 years earlier, he'd met the only woman
he'd ever be with, a woman who'd proven
to be a strong partner
how my sister & I were joys in his life
that he hoped he'd been a good father to us

I reminded him that he was not dying
he said he knew that, but of all the things
he wanted me to leave with that day
it was this knowledge, these words
that he wanted me to be nothing but happy

Dad's Wisdom

emails from my father
uncover new ground
my discovery of him
as writer

I see that he is careful with words
as these messages are significant
expressions of his pride for me,
my choices, my life

small truths are revealed
he writes, "mechanical things
do break down, just like people"
unexpected poetry

Letters in the Air

after Dad's surgery
as he lay in ICU with a breathing tube
he wanted to ask us how it went

to try to communicate
he used his finger as a pen
empty space as paper
to compose his words
letter by letter in the air

my sister & I did our best to read them
celebrating when he would nod 'yes'
apologizing when we guessed wrong

finally giving him the answers
he seemed so desperate to know

Winter Solstice 2017

on the longest night of the year
my father said he was ready to die

his decision was both shocking & comforting
we had talked on the phone earlier
he was desperately tired
it was different than other times

sitting beside him in his hospital room
my mom on the other side,
he said, "I've made a decision."
I took his hand, his skin soft & thin,
"I want to go home, be done with this,"
he gestured with his other hand to indicate
hospital, machines, gowns, fluorescence
"I want you to talk to them tomorrow."

after many tears & more talking
we left him to fall asleep unburdened
we called my sister to tell her, said we'd let her know
when we knew more about getting him home to start hospice

drive home was quiet, Mom & I
floating in a surreal landscape
everything shimmered, we were one beat behind

we spoke truthfully, tearfully
me admitting that I was writing poetry in my head
she admitting that she felt some relief
both of us feeling guilty for these thoughts
both of us forgiving the other for them
~~

that night, I slept in his bed,
but not before I examined his room,
opened closet doors
took a picture of his shirts
tried to sleep but could only see
a family vacation to Yellowstone
where he threw my child body into the air
so I could see higher, how I was surprised
then delighted by his spontaneity
the thrill of the toss, how he caught me
did it again, laughing
my daddy laughing
unburdened

Hospice Bubble Haiku

bubbles are short-lived
are fragile & beautiful
they float by quickly

Lift Team

the evening he came home, he told paramedics to put him
in his recliner in the living room
Mom made him something to eat
then she & I listened to the nurse
when he was ready for bed
Mom & I each got on a side,
put an arm underneath each of his armpits & lifted

in the morning, getting him from bed worked the same way
that night, when he was ready for bed,
my sister took over for my mom
on either side, we lifted him to his feet,
waited 'til he was steady enough to walk

he started calling us his lift team
whenever he needed to get from his bedroom
to the living room or back again
he called for us
the lift team had several members
but only two at a time for each lift

as days passed & family members had to go home
had to attend to their lives
my sister & I stayed with our mom & dad to attend to his dying
we noticed how much heavier he was getting
as fluid that was usually flushed out
through dialysis remained in his body

before long, we couldn't lift him

after paramedics were called to move him
we knew he'd have to stay in his room
we knew we'd have to tell him
but in a way that we all thought it was a good thing
we were the lift team

Poem From Inside His Hands

when the man takes to his bed
he starts on his left side
puts his left arm out so that
I am facing up, my palm exposed
sometimes I am slightly cupped
my other rests along his side

he likes to drift off with the blanket
pulled all the way over his exposed ear
a habit that his first daughter
recognizes as one she has herself
she seems both surprised & soothed
as the truth of it washes over her
she fixes him just so, gets his acknowledgement
that it's good, that he's comfortable

the other daughter, the second & last one,
watches this exchange, honors its importance
but she remains in the room, he asks for music
she facilitates that, adjusting volume
until again he acknowledges it's to his liking
then without fail, during these, the man's last days,
she slides her right hand into me & squeezes
I squeeze back & tears come to her eyes

she sometimes stays a moment more, whispers to him
caresses my skin gently, maybe trying to make sure
she doesn't forget the moment, unsure how many
more times she'll be able to slip her hand so easily
into my openness & squeeze, unsure how much
longer it will be until I can no longer squeeze back

Christmas Day

what I remember:
walking to Starbucks with my sister & her husband
tripping & falling flat on my face into a yard on the way home
when I told my dad I'd fallen, the way he took my hand,
patted it, chuckled a little
knowing it would be my dad's last Christmas
not knowing that when I'd purchased one of his gifts –
a 2018 page-a-day desk calendar
my dad requesting that we open our gifts, taking turns,
one by one, until we were done, then he would open his gifts
my nephew, surly & mumbly, a bit strung out, seemingly numb
to what was transpiring
the way my dad clapped & laughed
when I unwrapped my gift to him
when he went in for a nap, the way sun shone into his room
like it was just an ordinary day
George Jones loud on the stereo as he drifted to sleep
not being able to take one minute more in that house
calling B from drugstore parking lot to break down
wandering aisles of Walgreens, answering honestly when
cashier asked me how I was doing,
taken aback by his kindness,
embarrassed by my tears but unable to stop them
being grateful I was able to tell my dad
that it was my honor to help him

The Magical Cheeseburger

the day after Christmas
was Dad's 5th day at home
a Tuesday, it would have been
a dialysis day before, but instead
it was second appointment he missed

we followed our standard daily procedure
he rang his bell or called out
my sister or my mom & I
went into his room
brought him to a sitting position

sometimes he'd tell us what
he'd dreamed about, other days
he'd just smile & be happy
to have woken up

I can't remember when he
timidly asked me & my sister
if we would be too embarrassed
to help him get dressed, but we both
said we wouldn't so that became
a routine as well
he meticulously chose underwear, a t-shirt,
socks & a button-up shirt
to go with a pair of pajama pants

we went about getting him ready for his day
we got him into his chair in the living room
then he gave my sister his breakfast order
as he ate, we went for coffee or went about
our own morning routines
he watched TV or started talking,
telling stories of his life

on this day, we had a visit from Margarita,
a hospice nurse whose responsibility it was
to give Dad a bath, he was hesitant at first
but after she'd left, he was like a new man
he'd always been fastidious about being clean

for lunch, it was In-n-Out cheeseburgers all around,
with fries & shakes, as we ate, all of us commented
on how extra good the food seemed, like
divinely good, like the hamburger gods
knew what was going on in our corner
of the world & did their damnedest
to give us a beautiful memory of perfectly
grilled beef, remarkably melty cheese,
supremely soft buns

after lunch, Dad was ready for a nap
so we got him fixed in his bed, then his case nurse arrived
she took his blood pressure as we told her
about what had been going on, including
how he had just polished off his cheeseburger
like a champ
she was shocked, was even more surprised
by spike in his blood pressure

she proclaimed that this was all very unlikely
how that cheeseburger must have been
otherworldly, she said she wouldn't be back
for a few days because he was doing just fine
even though, given his issues, she would have
assumed otherwise

we laughed about it as Dad slept
as we wondered if we would, in fact,
soon have to face losing this man
or if it was something else completely,
if this might be the one time that a man
was brought back from the brink of death
by a cheeseburger

Caregiving

when Dad was released from the hospital
to come home for hospice
they insisted that he constantly be on oxygen
low, whirring concentrator in his room
before his trek to living room each morning,
then back again for naps & at night,
he'd ask for the cannula to be removed
afraid he'd get tangled in the tubing
I became an expert at reinserting it
into his nostrils, placing tubing up & over his ears

he asked me to help him put drops in his eyes
we did it in the living room, him reclining in his chair
I reached over him from behind, pinched skin
below his eye to make a cup, dropped in fluid
I was always afraid the pinch hurt him, but it never did

he asked me to rub lotion on his feet
he reclined, I sat on the floor
dispensed lemon-scented balm
gently applied it to his soft skin
he was lucky that the diabetes didn't affect his feet
he had fine feet
one time he scrunched up his shoulders
exclaimed, "Man, that feels so good!"

this care I provided was easy because it gave him comfort
the caregiving my mother did was different
while it also gave him comfort, it was the hard stuff
it was taking care of his abdominal colostomy
which was an open wound
that she managed like a pro for just about 6 years
cleaning, draining, changing
managing the bleeding

with him not going to dialysis, another issue came up
blisters, bigger than baseballs, began to form on his lower legs,
full of liquid, they would rupture & soak his pants
Mom began wrapping them so we wouldn't need to
keep changing his clothes

Dad was mostly stoic through it all
Mom was dutiful, doing these tasks
because she was the only one who could
she shielded us from the nasty reality of it,
but when I got a glimpse of it one night
I smothered her with a hug

when I was little, my dad would back up
to a doorjamb or a wall corner
move back & forth to get a good scratch
he reminded me of a bear

one night before bed
Mom & I sat on either side of him
fingernails moving gently across his back

Bequeathments

one afternoon, as winter sunlight waned
Dad asked me to bring a box from his room

small TV tray in front of him
he slowly began relieving box of its contents

rings, dog tags, a smaller box with papers
a couple bibles, ID cards

when everything was laid out
he asked me & my sister if we wanted anything

he picked up a gold ring, explained how Avi,
our Spanish grandfather, gave it to him

his initials intertwined
in raised letters on flat circle

another gold ring, Dixon High School,
class of '58, initials, ram's head

we each took a set of dog tags
we each took a bible

I also took the box of papers which held
drag race finishing times, army patches

my sister took Spanish ring
I took high school ring

I didn't start wearing it
until after

New Year's Eve/New Year's Day

we woke him just before midnight
glasses of champagne in hand
ready to toast the new year
whatever remaining days or hours
we would have together with him

champagne was cold, tangy
we closed our eyes as it slid down our throats
along with our bone-deep sadness
our tilted uncertainties
at least in that moment
because he was still with us
his blue eyes still seeing us
still able to tell us he loved us
as we got him back into bed
in early minutes of new year
—
when he said he didn't want breakfast
my sister & I shared a look
nurses had told us when we noticed
deviations in routine that it was a sign of transition
no breakfast was the second sign
the first was when he complained of chest pain
asked what narcotics we had in the house

in the kitchen I tried to remember
directions the nurse had given us
about dispensing morphine
I was overwhelmed with the task
almost couldn't do it, but knew I had to

instead of breakfast, he asked us to sit
with him, hold his hands, he asked
for a song by Dwight Yoakam,
something about miles from here
                        "A Thousand Miles from Nowhere"
then he asked me to play whatever
I liked in that vein
                  "Satisfied Mind"
                  "I'll Fly Away"
he asked if the saddles were put away
morphine working
he asked for The Blackwood Brothers
Sandy & I shared a laugh at its blatant Christianity
not typical for our areligious family
he remembered Sandy had made brownies
asked for one,

indicated he wanted me to keep the music going
I went through songs I knew would give me comfort
                              "This World is Not My Home"
                              "Will the Circle be Unbroken"
                              "Keep on the Sunny Side"
he shook his head gently back & forth
smiled a little, his ways of showing
his enjoyment & then he had another request,
he wanted to hear a singer he only knew as
Pat Boone's father-in-law,
web search brought up Red Foley
at the sound of the name, he clapped & said,
"That's him!"

Red owned the rest of the morning
my sister took a shower
Mom wandered in & out
I kept playing music
watched it soothe him
just as much as the morphine

did he give you a good story for the day he died?
—Lindsay White, "The Funeral"

when we could no longer lift him
when it took four paramedics to get him back to the bedroom
when he was barely able to verbalize
nurse told us to start giving him morphine every four hours
my sister & I made a deal that she would prepare the dropper
I would administer it
we began that night, 8 pm, 12 am, set our alarms, 4 am, 8 am

2nd day of the year
5th dialysis appointment missed
12th day within hospice bubble
Dad confined to his bed
he mostly slept, but when he would stir & grumble,
make discomforting noises or occasionally mutter
heartbreaking phrases like "help me,"
it almost always coincided with the next time for morphine

I would tell him I was giving him his medicine
he could hear & understand
he'd turn his head toward me, open his mouth slightly
so I could squeeze morphine into it, just inside his cheek
he would sometimes open his eyes, be comforted
I'd tell him I loved him, his mouth would move as if to answer

in the functioning world beyond us, it was back to work
because we couldn't think of anything else to do while he slept
my sister & I logged in to our respective offices

8 am, 12 pm, 4 pm, 8 pm, 12 am, set our alarms, 4 am

after 4 am administration of morphine
I couldn't go back to sleep
I kept checking on him, not disturbing him, but watching
his chest rise & fall with effort
shortly before 8 am, my sister said she heard him grumbling
with every four hours, I wanted another four & I didn't want it
I took the dropper, we went to his room
his chest no longer rose & fell
the bubble had burst
~~
the rest was easy & ridiculously difficult
the rest was peaceful & full of incomprehensible sadness
the rest was life goes on & everything's changed
the rest was feeling it all & feeling numb

my mom, sister & I sat on front steps
while the mortuary boys, who were just boys,
removed his body from the house

grey sky glared like sunshine off a mirror

The Hospice Bubble

slight as breath
delicate as onion skin
tenuous as a temp job
devastating as death

yet still protected
reinforced with family
strong with love
everlasting with memories
affirming as life

Dad's bubble was
comfort & peace
his siblings' prayer circles & story-telling
country music & cheeseburgers

we were his devotees
our only goals
shield him against pain
shepherd his last breath
with grace

No Funeral

when Dad first got very sick
he & my mother made their arrangements
Rose Hills would handle everything
cremation, simple details, nothing elaborate

I was uncomfortable in mortuary office
outside, a downpour, construction
everything felt temporary & grey

there were brochures about
releasing doves (which are
actually white homing pigeons),
memorial books, videos,
wakes, viewings, graveside services

we didn't want any of that
we weren't even planning a service
that was what they'd agreed on
~~
about a week into hospice
my dad was ready for a nap
he selected Willie Nelson for music
"Hands on the Wheel" came on
he told me that if we had a service
he wanted this song to be played
I simply agreed
knowing there would be no service
not because we didn't love him
or want to honor him, but
because this time was our service

nothing we could have planned
would have been as powerful or
as meaningful as it was to
hold his hand, kiss his face,
whisper "I love you" every time
he went to sleep

A Proper Heaven

1.
for you, Jeffrey Joe,
sun shines all the time
falls perfectly across your table
of course, there is music
guests who grace
your kitchen are people
whose music you've always
played, Hoagy Carmichael,
Nat King Cole, Hank Williams,
whoever else wanders by

you are light on your feet
have no pain
the true love you have for Carina
pulses from your big ol' heart
so that she feels it
when you need her to,
when she needs to feel it

2.
for you, Cathy,
a never-empty palette
every vista you've ever loved
Torrey Pines, Peñasquitos Lagoon,
road to Santa Ysabel & more
you cruise to them all
with your silver Airstream
set up your easel
with light always right

you never feel tired
you have no pain
you've got little Peanut
with you riding shotgun
your evening star
is ever shining
all is right with the world

3.
for you, Dad,
days that are neither too hot
nor too cold, but perfect for
sitting in patio swing
to watch hummingbirds, hear your chimes
you've reunited with your
parents & other loved ones
you're able to indulge
in all the watermelon Dad Moore
ever planted, tasty & big
listening to Grand Ol' Opry

or maybe it's a long, straight
road in Montana, you in
driver's seat of your
18-wheeler, Willie Nelson
on the radio, your left arm
hanging out window
honking air horn to little kids
who give you the signal
shades on, but no glare
never an empty tank

or maybe it's at the starting line
of a drag strip, you in
driver's seat of your 1958
B Gasser that you rebuilt yourself
clear sky of a summer night
rumble of motor as
you get green light
fly down raceway
always get checkered flag

your body is whole & healthy
you have no pain
you have perfect vantage point to see us
like always, you are proud of your girls

Picking Up the Ashes

my job granted three bereavement days
I used first one the day he died
second one was for the mortuary office,
the day we were required to confirm his identity,
an image of his face on a TV screen,
third day was when we picked up the ashes

Rose Hills in Whittier, California
is a sprawling area where generations
have been laid to rest, thousands of tears
have been shed, where my mom & I
headed on a sunny January day
to retrieve the cremains of my father

we spoke quietly to receptionist
waited quietly in expansive lobby
watched quietly as people came in,
finely dressed, to attend a viewing
or a funeral, participate in their personal
rituals to honor their dead

finally, an attendant approached
carrying a bag which she placed
in front of us, said she had to see
about flag we requested
due to him being a veteran,
she asked that we confirm his name

Mom looked in the bag, saw gold box,
size of a large book, sticker with his name
on the end, where the pages would be
she confirmed that it was him
when we were alone again, we each picked
up the bag, surprised at its weight

the flag was given to us
already folded, encased in a
soft, plastic, triangular holder
I took it, Mom took the bag
we brought him home
placed box & flag in his room

we'd talked about places we could
spread the ashes, had talked to him
early on about his wishes
nothing was finalized
Mom didn't think she wanted
to keep the ashes in the house

she has changed her mind

Lung Point

I discovered a bruise
when I pulled my shirt off
at bedtime

I was surprised when I saw it
by its darkness, shape, location –
a narrow horizontal oval
on my upper left bicep
I thought back to what could have caused it

I realized I'd had an acupuncture
needle in that spot earlier, but
it was curious because
I've never bruised before

at my next appointment
I explained the bruise
I had already reconciled it
as some anomaly, nothing significant

then she told me that had been
a new point she had placed,
lung point, also known as
grief point

a beat passed

in that space, the mental movie
of losing my dad just under 3 months before
flashed through my brain
I never considered that
grief could manifest
as a marker on my skin
temporary tattoo
of my sadness

This is a True Story

Larry liked to talk of death,
whether he realized it or not,
he had many anecdotes about it

there was the boulder that
crashed down a mountain
into a Greyhound bus traveling
two-lane road, killing
some passengers
the boulder so big, they left it
where it landed
split in two, one part on side
of the road, other part
in the Rio Grande

there were the drug deaths in Española
young girls & boys who overdosed

his own stories of near death
from being in the mining accident
that almost cost him his legs
to car crash that killed his brother

as we neared Taos
gorge to our left, he told of
girls who had jumped from bridge
he asked why I thought they did that
I was too busy counting up scenarios
he had already illustrated of tragic deaths

he had no way of knowing of my recent experiences
no reason to believe that grief would be
at my very surface
but this is how I walk the earth for now
one part in celebration, spirited
one part mourning spirits

Other Devastating Affirmations

Death

Dixon, CA Pop. 13,708

rows of oaks shelter rain-soaked road
from nor'wester blowing
gentle seeds across my grandparents' graves

bones of dogs have been tilled into soil
crows crown walnut trees in afternoon
buzzards feast in middle of the road

there is no sadness
where there should be sadness
a chair empty many years
but still turned out to receive her
echoes of him asking for some sugar

their love lined in every quilt
stacked six high in cedar closet

Great Uncle

maps of Arizona
remind me of
something I've
never written
but have only
followed silently
with my finger
traced it like
a gravel road
through a national park

a farmer's truck
parked in my driveway
is soil of my blood
is a dead man's fingerprints
still on steering wheel
footprints on floorboards
coated with 14 year old dust
of barley & wheat fields

it's the truck
I will drive
to Arizona
on gravel roads
the dead man & I
will guide it
over poems
not yet written
we will slice
through heart
of direction
split north from south
dress wounds
with memories
of morning conversation
though neither of us
can remember
the other's voice

*In my heart I hold your photograph and the thought of you
comes on like the feel of the coming rains*
—Bruce Cockburn, "The Coming Rains"

morning was overcast
as we headed north on interstate 5
toward Marysville

it was 2nd day of the year
we were going to his father's funeral

we were quiet
still processing emotions
that were handed to us
so suddenly
when this song came on

something shifted in the air
as we locked into the words
& wept
~~
a couple months later
we sat in a parking lot
in Austin

suddenly, here was this song again
we both remembered
last time we'd heard it

this time he pointed out a favorite line
about smoke sliding into a room
then fell quiet
& wept

Swimming in the Sky
for Nancy

horizon is indiscriminate
unsure where sky ends
or ocean begins
they blend together
as if they were one

so you dive in & realize
gravity has reversed

you doggy paddle —
work to avoid
sharp rays of sun
that hide in marine layer
that seek to sting you

you catch wing
of passing raven
let it do the work
as you keep your head below
cloud cover

strong stroke
takes you across
arc of the day

finally, you ride meteors like waves
across atmosphere
trail hand through stars
leaving a wake of shimmers

Sky Search

flying west toward California
toward home
golden horizon beckons
promising nothing

we hurtle through sky
at death-defying speeds
through unimaginable cold
in relative comfort

I start reading a new book
about a woman who loses her job
creates plans to start a mobile bookshop
it is near to my dream but farther away than hers

I wonder if it's a sign to follow my dreams
song in my ears is about flying "Into the Sun"
same thing I am doing at the moment
song changes to "Almost Home"
another signal of my present moment

sky slowly turns to dusk
while horizon remains a fiery dark orange

I consider how I knew when her name
came up on my phone that she was gone
it was her sister calling, I took comfort
in her voice, which was so similar to her sister's,
much like my sister's voice & mine confuse people
the sister confirmed she died as sun rose

outside this celestial time machine
light stretches its arms toward me, growing fainter

one of the last times I saw her, we held hands
on her bed, stared at one of her paintings
of the sky in the gloaming with an evening star
glowing brightly in the center - "That's where
I'm going," she said. So matter-of-factly, so positive.

I glance out portal window as plane descends
searching sky to spy a glimmer of her spirit
to gather courage to follow the signs

For Jeff Buckley

rivers that run through Memphis
will take you down
swallow your arms, your bare feet
all the loveless parts of you

you have no say against it

your voice means nothing to the river
the earth wants you inside it
the river is the mouth
that will take you down
take you in
learning every inch of you
committing you to memory
like none of your lovers ever could

only amid the water's chaos
will you feel true tenderness
as roaring becomes the only sound
bigger than you
bigger than you could ever know sound could be
nothing can save you

you are being called to the edges
to void of aching silence & extreme anger
that can only be soothed by the river

in Memphis, where you were quiet,
creative, unheard
where you fought lack of love
loss of tenderness
turned it into grace
fabric of a simple city dress
ageless, ageless

you made demands only rivers could answer

it approached you with intention
like none of your lovers ever could

To a Ghost

find your flesh again
bits & pieces wait
in creases of books
stretch over empty canvases
glow dimly in light fixtures
sit motionless on
edge of windowsill
collect them all slowly
locate spaces where they
belong over your bones

your skin slowly
stitches itself back together

pull it down
over your neck & arms
roll it smoothly
into place
over your chest & hips
let gravity help it
cover your legs

examine it now carefully
it is intricate, strong

stand in your flesh again
breathe
feel the ground
beneath your bare feet
run your fingertips along
smooth & quiet
branches of a city tree
angle your mouth
around top of a pen

feel heat warm your body that was
draped over a desk
left empty in misshapen pile
on the dance floor
prostrate between pews

greet me whole again
solid wrists & firm ankles
kiss my mouth
breathe
while we stand together
revive more ghosts

My Ophelia

I found myself at the ocean on a windy night
followed a road I usually do not travel
considered descending stairs
to inch my way along cliffs
if I should slip, then I might fall
so what of that

wind whipped at my eyes
so I could not stare long
at darkness
that screamed at me

maybe it was the same night
that you, dressed in lily white
with flowers hanging 'round
your face, got closer than I did
lay yourself down on hard sand
twisted your body
did not think
only accepted
water coming slowly higher
at your ankles, then knees

cold

your hand brushed across your face
covered it with sand
flowers from your hair
fell in front of you
into ocean
out to their death
where yours waited
not speaking

cold

you became aware of one thought
that you would miss rainy days
this was enough
to turn you around
get you to bed
breathing

this strange experience
now yours
but also mine
with our dresses heavy
with their drink
floating face upward
violets & pansies clutched in our fists
rosemary dripping through
our fingers like saltwater & sand

we travelled down our roads
but we found a way home
breathing

my Ophelia
we have not yet had our fill

Depression

Lessons

there is something to be said for simple
easy laughter, a song you like on the radio
a clear sky, a bright orange sunset

on these nights, when it's quiet
& sleep comes without asking
it's important to acknowledge

because elsewhere,
or maybe even here tomorrow
it won't be like this

there's something to be said for difficult
tough conversations, terrible news on the radio
stormy skies, darkness of a starless night

on these nights, when it's too much to take
& sleep is nowhere to be found
it's important to acknowledge

because elsewhere,
or maybe even here tomorrow
it won't be like this

Those first days...she always found herself alone when the weather broke.
—Michael Ondaatje, *Anil's Ghost*

it is not quite summer
& she is distracted
her clothes tumble
for 10 minutes
for only 25 cents
she remembers
watching him untie his new lover's scarf
the relief of her neck
where he would bury his face later
weather changes
in such small moments

she reaches her right hand
over her left shoulder
presses her fingers into muscles
of her back
this is where her storms begin & end

she has memorized the location
massages it when she feels clouds gathering
it is where she directs her chaos
as if you can control the hurricane
as if the knowledge of its arrival
will somehow make you safer

A Girl I Know

when she closes her eyes
she sees sun spots
that bloom into sunflowers

she tilts her head back
looks up to tall green stalks
brown centers wink at her

when she opens her eyes
clouds are scattered
like buckshot across the sky

deep down she believes
she's not particularly good at anything
but sometimes she surprises herself

water is metallic in her mouth
so she thinks she is losing her humanity
she cries at confrontation & heartfelt gestures
so we know she is not

she is not winsome or light
though she wishes like hell she could be one day
wearing sundresses & drinking bourbon in late September

till then she'll stare into the sun
close her eyes & disappear
into a field of sunflowers

How to Bring Her Back

put feathers to the winds to guide her
through elements & directions
        (she stumbles through
        Sioux Falls blizzards
        for weak coffee & warm soup)

light candles & sing siren songs
        (she wants to come home)

summon magic of familiars to lay before her
        (she hovers)

weep rivers for her to sail back to intimate shores
        (she writes letters on backs of useless maps)

gather hazel for reconciliation & flowering almond for hope

she wants to learn how to be hungry again

Hole in the Floor Mat

my driver's side floor mat
has a hole where
my right heel has
worried through fabric

I don't know how
long my heel has
worked to accomplish
this feat

I have noticed it
slowly growing
I have rearranged
floor mat to
slow its growth

but it always
inches back
to spot
where my heel
rests in hole
~~
what else in my life
has sustained such
pressure to have altered
its appearance

what part of me
has such sustained
pressure to cause
that alteration
~~
for some
pressure
is intangible

for some
intangible
is pressure

Break

I wait for something to break
condemned buildings & rusted out cars
someone pulls the plug
someone pulls a trigger

I wait for some extreme measure
to knock me around, compel me
to find balance in things
I worry I take for granted

I wait for a seismic shift
in my topography
for ridges to crumble
mountains to flatten

I wait for a hurricane
to cut through my insides
leave empty space
force me to rebuild

I wait for a flood
to wash through me
wipe out everything
but the foundation

I wait for a wildfire
to burn away structure
so only memories remain

I fear these invocations
of natural disasters unleashed
on heart & soul

when they arrive
they frighten me at first
but eventually
earth stops shaking
wind dies down
water ebbs
embers cool
my feelings subside
numbness returns

Phantoms & Flights

my life is strikingly devoid of phantoms

there's a ghost in the house across the street
but she doesn't bother me

I say "she" because it seems to be a neighborhood of women
who live long
who outlive their lovers
who fold sheets by themselves in their living rooms
who sing softly to shadows
sit barefoot on their porches

she is a quiet ghost
picks up her paper in the mornings
turns off her light at night
she doesn't care to share her ghostliness with any of us

the planes never stop coming down
in the distance they remind me of thunder
as they near, they change to long deep moaning,
a suffering like the last body-wracking sobs of a breakdown
volume of approach consumes sky
screams of deliverance
birth & crossing over in flight

I wait & listen for any phantoms to echo
but none do
she, across the street, remains quiet
as if she has no obligation to answer
does not notice it anymore

Hawks & Sunsets

that sunset was mine alone
& tonight the hawks are everywhere

as shadows begin their takeover
red-tails perch atop light poles along freeway
scan brush for prey
the way my eyes tracked sun in its descent
as if my life depended on it

because it does

I must pay attention to the way light changes
to vigilant hawks
it's important that I take stock of myself
notice my breathing & how I feel in my own skin
because if I don't
I will drown in my depression
that is masked as detachment more & more these days

if I continue to lose touch with myself
my panic attacks, that offer no warnings, will paralyze me

there's a moment as my hyperventilating & sobs
begin to subside
when I feel suspended
I know there are options

I could dive like the hawk intent on a kill
but without any power over my wings
crash hard so it all starts over again

or I could gingerly, blindly, reach out to a guide
one who is home to me
to help me find my footing
remind me to concentrate on my breath
in through the nose, out through the mouth
deliberate, rhythmic
that option puts me on solid ground again
numbness slowly builds like brambles to protect me
until next time

Moon Shine

last night I kept blinds open
unconcerned about who might see into my bedroom
spy fading tan on my bare breasts
full harvest moon brightly lit up my darkened room
I somehow desperately needed to
fall asleep in the moon shine
my body craved its cleansing luster
my mind calmed under its brilliance
~
come October, I'm usually ready for
scary movies & creepy stories
you know: being afraid of a madman
on the loose, feeling terrified of what
he might do, always on edge of an
impending apocalypse & its aftermath

but these days, fear is engrained in
every hour, especially for
women
Muslims
Dreamers
the sick
Mexicans
African-Americans
Jewish people
the press
those who identify as LGBTQ
scientists
Gold Star families
immigrants
students
Native Americans
natural disaster survivors
veterans
athletes
"others"
it's worse if you are a
combination of any of the above

all of this insanity, this never-ending
temper tantrum, this perverse power play
by a grossly inept & narcissistic hairdo is
enough to keep my hackles raised & my
fight or flight response on constant alert
~

so you understand why when that moon
made its presence known, it was
almost automatic to bask in it, pearly
translucence overtaking shadows

I chose to use it to conjure peace
I summoned all my familiars to serve as
protection, invited spirits to watch
over me & mine, casted spells of
love, health & joy knowing the moon
would make them solid, would make them
grow whole, would make them come to pass
like the burn of moonshine down your throat

Bone Songs

there is an ache
somewhere near
bottom of my throat
base of the neck
that is a sad song
played outdoors
near water

there is a tremble
in my chest
that is the difference
between love
& lover

there is a hollow
at center of my stomach
where heights drop
depths rise
leaving me unbalanced

there is a half-moon
at edge of my fingernails
that reminds me
of dead blues

there is a sigh
twisting from my ankles & wrists
gurgling from my blood
trying to expel my exhaustion

Murders, Unkindnesses & Other Winged Things

I've got a thing for birds
not just any birds, but certain ones
those steeped in mythology or magic
ones that signal omens & fate

that said, most birds frighten me
I have only recently begun
to enjoy whoosh of hummingbirds
as they dive & swoop
toward feeder in my parents' backyard
their impossibly fast, tiny wings
fluttering like a feeling my heart used to know
but when a hummingbird is still
it's like being let in on a secret

birds of prey are magnificent
hawks, falcons, owls
enormous wingspans & mighty talons
even Zeus chose an eagle as his companion
but always crows & ravens
have enchanted me
even their collective nouns conjure mystery

a murder of crows
bringers of light & death
godlike & wise
but always up for a good joke
they hold memories of other worlds
their familiar caws make my mornings

an unkindness of ravens
known to pick on other species
as a group if necessary
highly intelligent
symbolic of mind & thoughts
straight from myth of Odin

I have dreams where I fly
I am neither crow nor raven
but the higher I go, the lighter I feel
to escape from daily
murders & unkindnesses
that we know
that we mourn
that we rage against
that don't go away
when we close our eyes

No Man's Land

3 am is a no man's land
dark as raven's wings
quiet as a broken bell

it is insomnia's playground
merry-go-round of the mind
won't stop spinning

synapsing swings
tangled chain link
rattles brain

sleeplessness teams up with time
they chase dreams away
like ghosts taking control
of their haunting

it's not long before
madness starts to breed

it begins with raven's eye
reflecting split clapper
blinks, then delirium
lies flat on its back
imagines it's turning the world
on that ceaseless carousel
to soundtrack
of rusty steel couplings
swaying back & forth
then hysteria comes
with barrage of bothersome banshees
swarm of swirling spirits

sleep fights through
morning breaks

December Sleep

my sickness & solitude's coupling
brought forth fevers
that now as offspring
visit me yearly
like good yet distant
grandchildren
who do not send letters
or postcards
just show up
expecting love
like children do

I reluctantly welcome them
hope they won't unpack their bags
I know are stuffed
with death dreams
they will try to give me
like gifts
like candy

we play games
with each other
try to scare
each other
to death
I discover that
their only fear is fire
it is too much
their origin
holds too many memories
of home
I keep my body warm
pour hot liquids over & into me
stay near flames

my weakness
is my sleep
when all defenses
are down
these babies of fire
sneak into my room
with their suitcases
crawl into my bed
quietly release
those dreams

Figure at a Window, 1925
after painting by Salvador Dali

in my last conversation with Saturn
I could sense retreat

never completely turning his back on me
I know he's edging away

footfalls silent as a shadow
eyes blue as the sea

you may not understand
but there is always benevolence nearby
regardless of his position

call it awareness or insight
but he demands structure
through every challenge
or creative effort

I must keep peace
close at hand

so it comes to this

easy linen, still water
something like wisdom
helps support this weight

everything that brought me to this point
leans in with me

Emergence

a fingertip
a strand of hair
an eyelash
my pinkie toe

ever so slowly
it seems
I may just find
my way out

Writing

One Way Rain

it is the way of the rain
airborne ocean moves in waves
keeps coming
changes course
like tide follows moon
these drops & grey clouds
suggest the season
will witches show themselves
will phantoms slip through crack
for Samhain

I heard voices in quiet church
I saved myself from thirst
by sucking rain from my hair

like going out in it
soft cotton & clean socks
my paper wet & ink running down pages

like coming in out of it
stolen motel towels hang clean
I pretend I'm on the road
empty suitcases on living room floor
strangers argue in the street
new neighbors sleep with old friends
hard luck losers hit a winning streak
pages already full of years
opened after just as long
where my stories spell out
your loving, his hardness, her tears

Leo rising & hands travel texture of my hair
make their wishes on silver & turquoise
drops of pearls fall from curls
twist & smooth themselves into bands
around my fingers

so now you know the animal
have seen yourself differently
in shadows of moonlight

it is the way of the rain
night is a jack o'lantern
grinning like a drunken wise man
ready to share his last bottle
& all he knows

Poet Out of Practice

sometimes it feels like my best words are behind me
I shuffle through old poems, re-reading them
it seems like I barely know woman who wrote those lines
wonder if I could come close to capturing details
that once seemed so easy to notice

to get back in the swing of things
I write out recipes on little note cards
slowly remember flow of refreshing ink onto thirsty paper
return of language, its descriptive nature,
urges me on as I continue with my exercise
re-discovering verbs that move like
boil, brush, spoon, toss, cover, melt
adjectives that entice like
zesty, warm, wild, blackened, spicy

small, forgotten ache begins to stir in my hand
I ponder mechanics of writing, the way fingers
flex to grip pen, how wrist endures
slow dragging across page
how muscles that allow such action begin near elbow

I put down pen for a moment, rub my forearm gently
slowly rotate my wrist, release joints in my fingers
hear clear snap like onion hitting hot oil

capturing recipes returns me to language
comforting memories of fingertips
scented with garlic, faint hints of basil, tomato

like a sidelined athlete needs to get back on the court
or musician needs to rehearse,
the very task of writing anything encourages
the poet out of practice

Grace

she lives here with me
but she comes & goes as she pleases

never tells me where she's going
never leaves a note

it's typical that she'll come in
just as I'm falling asleep

I catch glimpses of her sometimes
usually when there's music

we used to be inseparable
I didn't think she'd ever leave

now, daily happenings of my life
rarely interest her

but sometimes they do
then she'll spend time with me

when that happens
I remember how good it feels

her company is like an avalanche of
warm towels just out of the dryer

I could stay there all day

The Best Poem I Ever Wrote

I scribbled some words about
love stories & growing old
when wine took me over

I slept easily, used full length
& width of my bed, didn't
curl up snug but spread out
my limbs, like a bird in flight,
like a fearless child

in the morning, I moved
at sluggish pace
of my hangover

no headache, but a sweet taste
in my mouth, a slow mind
in a rapid world
as details of my condition
came pouring back over me

I vaguely recalled writing something
I became eager to see
what I had captured,
like a trapper wishing for a mink

I picked up pages, read about
love stories & growing old
love that goes beyond death
to tell its story on tombstones

my eyes suddenly
dropped down to notice
a long black stain
on my flannel pajama bottoms,
spots on my shirt

with further investigation,
smaller stains on my skin & in my sheets
where I found the pen, left uncapped

I slept in a pool of black ink,
that stained nearly everything but the page,
& that long, black, permanent stain
is my best poem

Letter to a Blue Moon

I remember last time you were here
close enough that I could feel
your touch at my shoulder
how you slipped down strands of my hair
to swing & play at the ends
it was July
you sent rain ahead of you then too

I watched it roll across valley
in its stagecoach of dark clouds
thunder the same sound
as horses at a gallop

I send no such signals
to announce my arrival
but I suppose since you're so rare
it is appropriate,
a way to make us notice

since that last time
I've written a lot of poems
done some traveling
maybe somewhere
you've already seen
whose names are written in stone
whose are written in water

the other day,
I noticed that when I floss
my mouth feels bigger
more capable
& I've begun to formulate
theories regarding
how your dreams are influenced
by quilts you sleep under

you should really try to come around more often
but I understand the call of hermitage
the desire for aloneness

I hope you'll keep rain
as a companion on your visits
you both are always welcome here

p.s.
I saw you this morning still
hanging around like a boy
with a crush

Love

Close

my mother likes where she lives
because she knows she could go
to downtown LA whenever she wants
because it's not that far

she rarely goes to downtown LA
but that's not the point
she just likes knowing she could
because it's there

I have similar feelings
about people I love
though it feels dangerous
like I'm setting myself up to lose

Camouflage

shower's on to mask
small sounds
snores, sobs, sighs of passion

TV's on, so are the lights
to make it look like someone's home
when we're really nowhere close
off anyplace else in a hotel room somewhere

stereo's turned up loud
to cover din of an argument
fueled by volume
static hiss of a bad frequency

we talk in apologetic whispers
barely over sound of washing machine
that spins & cleans
makes things seem new again

my heart is not one for disguises
hard to conceal from hunters
vulnerable to capture
in plain view for gatherers & healers
open to enchantment
& what lies hidden in your touch

a hard cry could draw walls in, it could bend metal, it could turn a full moon into a sliver
—Sarah Addison Allen, *The Sugar Queen*

not as much as before
not like it used to be
tears enough to drown in
sorrows fit for a crone

but aftermath produced
no supernatural redemption, no relief
just fatigue

slow unrolling
of hours, lists of
ingredients for recipes
that will maybe
get made, wait on
stovetop for others
to maybe eat

waiting to give in
to sleep, to hear
one or another return
not call out to me
the awkwardness
seemingly too much
to overcome

if only the sobs
could have broken
open more than
just my heart

if only the weeping
could have been
a baptism, a beginning
rather than the exit
sign that finally lit up

Novice Masons

the house was falling down all around them
plaster peeling, cracks snaking up walls
sinkhole under bathroom that
threatened every morning

the house's ramshackle state –
its drooping doorways, its leaky roof, its drafty windows –
was like the relationship housed inside it

they were all in disrepair
just in need of the proverbial tender loving care
but day-to-day toil
melancholy of routine
effort to withstand wear & tear
was proving a tough adversary

they left the house behind

it remained vacant for years, as if others
had heard of its contagious decrepitude
its windows yawned its loneliness

the relationship fits into new spaces
rebuilds, repairs, compresses, expands
not without its imperfections, but easier to accept
not as dangerous
they are careful to try & fix cracks they create
before they fall apart

Contractors

the next house required some specialization
custom rooms created
money well spent

it was solid
they filled it with music
friends, family

but later, other visitors arrived
death, panic, disease
unwelcome but lingering
unseen but felt
invisible tendrils of damage
doing destructive work on the(ir) foundation
that they were unprepared to fix
that they were not skilled enough to repair

Master Builders

I.
work continued
each with ideas of their own
which sometimes overlapped
but often did not

this new home
quirkier than the last
but more suited to them in ways
both wanting to believe that
after years of toil
this one would be their masterpiece

but they failed to see
rats in the trees
suspicious neighbors
they failed to comprehend
isolation they'd feel
from friends, from family, from each other

deck went unswept
dust collected on everything
feeble attempts at cleaning
or somehow trying to make it better
were abandoned

II.
there had been warnings for months
maybe even years if you were following along

the flood was a ruination
the flood was a revelation
the flood signaled a turn

our builders put down their tools
one at a time
each deciding in their own way
to stop working on the façade

Holidays

she was hugging a woman
(the second she had wanted
to kiss full on the lips)
when she was told
she smelled like a memory

Christmas Eve
she picked lemons
from her parents' tree
rubbed Mexican & pineapple sage leaves
between her fingers
ran her earth-stained hands
through her hair
over her mouth

miles south
milk soured in her refrigerator
& doors remained closed
on her advent calendar
a forgotten December ritual
a scent of chocolate
on her breath

The Girl Who Dreamed of Bees

sunlight swarms into her room
while she presses sleepy hands into her eyes
pushes hair casually from her face

she begins to tell me her dream about bees
comes alive
busily working out details
faint, soft scent of lemon
rises from her skin
white down comforter
slips from her naked body

I am drawn to curve
of her hip, smooth as a flower petal
I slide my hand over it

we share these pure moments like honey

she is at the point in the dream
where the bees sting her
they are, of course, also drawn to her
sweetness, to her unashamed beauty

she wonders what it all means
but I know that she is like the Melissae
they are this goddess's companions
as she continues to discover
power of their medicine

I leave her
curved & warm in her bed
my mind still buzzing
with thoughts of her skin

The Ballad of Richard & Mildred

let's talk about love
let's talk about loving
a young woman
loves a young man
they share each other's
most significant spaces
sweet intimacies create a baby
they choose to marry
but Richard is white
Mildred is African-American,
part Rappahannock
it is 1958 in Virginia
where their love
is miscegenation & illegal

this is about love
this is about loving
they go to D.C. where
that law doesn't exist
they marry, they go back home
a month later
as they sleep
in their wedded bliss
police raid their house
hope to catch them
in another illegal act
are disappointed when they don't
Richard & Mildred are arrested
put in jail
to avoid their one-year sentence
they agree to leave their home in Virginia
for 25 years

this is about love
this is about loving
for five years, they live away from home
travel secretly back & forth
to visit their families
finally Mildred has enough
she writes to Robert Kennedy
he refers her to the ACLU
they take the case
file a motion that their sentence
violates 14th amendment
they go all the way to the Supreme Court

this is about love
this is about loving
on June 12, 1967
a unanimous decision
concludes miscegenation laws
are racist

this is about love
this is about Richard & Mildred
who were not radicals
they were just in love
had a family
wanted basic right
to live together as husband & wife
regardless of color of their skin

this is about love
this is about Richard & Mildred
this is about Mr. & Mrs. Loving

Sins & Miracles

I am wearing Las Vegas home
white cotton steeped in beer,
sweat, residue of bed sheets,
memories of cigarettes whose
ghostly smoke still found ways
into these fibers
that now surround
my own sins & miracles

it was in Las Vegas
where we finally did not touch,
exchanged no compliments,
did not accept our anger
or loneliness

July heat took away my sense of responsibility,
value of a dollar,
but made me believe again
in wet skin
like christening
even this defeated clothing
offers protection against
glowing presence risen from flatland

but you ignore danger,
continue to sacrifice
your gift of common sense,
self-imposed limitations
you check your definition of moderation
at state line,
maybe hide it away in your trunk,
believe it will be easy to bring it out again,
but Las Vegas does not let you
get away so quickly

so now I'm wearing Las Vegas,
covered in its desert heat
stains from quarters
on my fingertips like scars,
like those moments
we finally did not come together,
could not absolve each other
of our personal, unspeakable
sins & miracles

Aero-Dynamics

he likes to know what the sky is doing
to understand movement of wind
its origin or its destination
how it sweeps down from Alaska into California
over to Texas
brings winter

when it approaches
he wants to know if he should keep his door locked against it
or maybe leave door ajar, to let whatever forces come in
or if he should swing it open wide
so winds have to cross his threshold
to get where they're going
re-shape his living in the process

he is aware of air traffic over Los Angeles
lights line the sky
mark a pattern of arrival
against fixed outlines of myths

he notices shapes of clouds
how they are lit from western sunlight
points them out to me as a reminder of everyday poetry

he curves his arm around my waist
like arc of a plane on final approach

My Pleasure

it has been my pleasure
to receive love poems
not intended for me
at least not as the subject matter
but for a careful eye
a critic to help him
better define his love for another

it has been my pleasure
to be told my company
is no longer wanted because
I was not the friend that she expected

it has been my pleasure
to sleep easily *en la cama de mi abuela*
where they say she died like a bird

it has been my pleasure
to witness Sunset Blvd at midnight
where there are five dreamers for every one dream
with little difference between the revolution
& the common tide

it has been my pleasure
to suffer the realization
that I may be just ordinary

it has been my pleasure
to watch every erratic & gentle arrow
volley back & forth
drunk on the music between us

Letter Writing #1

I drive barefoot
jump from the truck
to post a letter
to a house in South Dakota
with columns
drawn in charcoal,
deep bath waters,
long hair wet & waving
like the prairies
colors of your skin

I don't check to see if letter
has safely slid down
angled blue federal metal

I am trusting that way

Letter Writing # 3

envelope corners
where my truths try to hide
like between my fingers
bends of my elbows
behind my knees
where lies cannot survive
in earthy darkness of my skin
you slowly unfold every crease
to expose my philosophies
I trust strangers to deliver parts of me
I trust thinnest strip of glue
to keep all that truth in one place
locked up until you slice across top
or slowly tear down side
until I finally spill out into your rooms
travelled so far these words
all the breath that escaped me
to reach you

Letter Writing #5

he said it is a lost art
this taking pen to paper
but for me it is not only
crafted sentences
interesting stories
I send to you
but I bend my whole body
into these words
range of my emotions
fits surprisingly well
into a small rectangle
that I seal safely
with quiet liquid of my mouth

Midnight Lesson

so we go to common ground
do not sit close
remark on the weather
go no deeper

this is how I learn
this is how I understand
placement
how lines are drawn

The Window
after painting by Marc Chagall

storms move like wars & love affairs
cloudy with bursts of blue sky & reason
they roll over land & sea, leave their mark
hearts & souls imprinted for a moment
or a lifetime
sometimes they begin without warning
or maybe you've seen them approaching
uncertain of their intentions
or whether you will come through them
without injury
perhaps you know of no way to protect yourself
so you face them bravely
but if you can, seek occasional shelter
a place to go where you can ride them out
those who study them
will be best prepared
when they are repeated

The Breath Before Hallelujah

you call on something greater than you
you say "Smother this room with light
& let me be unharmed."

there are different ways we burn
little fires that start
when your hands are in my hair
invisible sparks of secrets

hang your sorrowful dreams in my attic
already papered with purple shadows
of nightmares I've released to walls
spoken their truths like a prophet
with a fiery tongue

I call on something greater than you
I say "Help me tend the fire
& let me be unharmed."

I burn in ways that cause little damage
small flames that smolder
at a constant rate
release aromas of my secrets

I hang honeysuckle & lilac in my rooms
built slowly from fantasy & natural light
of Sunday mornings spilling wisdom
like water that soothes
my fiery tongue

Season's End

first season of living was winter
life started in its dark hours
moved slow among shadows
breathing still as time passed

when I feel light now these past mornings
I think on this first season that has passed
fallen into memory
like lovers

of course I sense natural lightening of earth
can almost touch the hope
that seems to drift
against my wide front door
& new ways afternoon spills
into this room, now in its new season,
remind me of old poems,
dusty magic & how your body felt
against mine that morning

when I walk to get coffee
ease of this lightness pours over me
even like the way sun will burn hard
into wood, worn & beautiful,
that sings me to sleep at night

the trick is to shine & not burn
to have & not to hold

Acknowledgements

Proper credit & my utmost gratitude is owed to the fine editors of these anthologies who previously published poems contained in this book, some in slightly different forms:

51%; Beyond the Valley of Contemporary Poets; Comstock Review; Don't Blame the Ugly Mug; Driftwood Highway; San Diego Poetry Annual; Savage Melodies & Last Call Serenades; Sheila-Na-Gig; So Luminous the Wildflowers; A Theater of Poets, Act 1; A Year in Ink, volumes 2 & 10

Previous versions of some poems were published in these self-published chapbooks:

Naked Wrists
12 Windows

Some poems were published in *Complicated Skies* published by The Inevitable Press (Laguna Poets Series #119)

"Patricia Said..." was inspired after seeing Patricia Smith perform "When the Burning Begins"

"Poem from Inside His Hands" & "A Proper Heaven" were written after prompts from Rachel McKibbens.

Thanks to Barbara, Lindsay, Becky & Mike who helped me walk through grief with what I hope is a small measure of grace.

Thank you to those who, maybe unwittingly, helped inspire me to write, to speak, to speak out, to cry, to love, to get help & to live.

Deep thanks & ever-loving gratitude to my mom, Josefa; my sister, Sandy; all of our family; & most especially to my dear departed Daddy-O, Alonzo Marvin Wann.

About the Author

Lizzie Wann graduated with a BA in Literature/Writing from UC San Diego where some of her professors included Victor Hernandez Cruz, Fanny Howe & Quincy Troupe. When she saw Patricia Smith perform as part of "Artists on the Cutting Edge" in La Jolla, she was hooked on mixing performance with the power in the written word. She started attending open mics around Southern California, became the San Diego scene reporter for *Next...* magazine, created her own readings & produced original shows that featured poets & musicians. She earned a spot on the 1999 Laguna Beach national slam team that competed at the National Poetry Slam in Chicago of that year, & from there, helped make slam poetry a San Diego fixture. She hosted one-off slams, then co-hosted the fledgling San Diego slam, then held at the Urban Grind, until 2003. She also founded the Meeting Grace house concert series which ran from 2000-2008. Her work appears on 2 CDs (A Wing & A Prayer – nominated for Best Local Recording for the 2000 San Diego Music Awards – & A New Leaf), in chapbooks & in anthologies.